WomWom is ready to explore. She is going to look at plants.

WomWom eats plants and grasses for food. She drinks water.

Plants need food and water to grow. Plants use light from the Sun to grow.

WomWom eats many different plants for food. WomWom can eat vegetables like carrots.

Plants are food for many living things. Insects and animals both need plants.

Butterflies eat the nectar in flowers. WomWom sees flowers but does not eat them.

WomWom looks at some roots and dead plants. These break down to form compost.

WomWom finds earthworms in compost. Earthworms eat dead plants. Earthworms leave dung in the compost.

Farmer Addy puts the compost on the ground. The compost helps the trees grow.

WomWom gets rid of the waste food in her body by making dung. WomWom leaves dung on the grass. The dung helps the grass grow.

Water helps the plants to grow. Water can fall from the clouds. WomWom stays in her burrow when it rains.

Water can come from clouds as snow or rain. WomWom does not like rain. Snow turns into water when it melts.